SIMPLE TRUTH

The Whole is Greater Than the Sum of Its' Parts

RALPH A. MORGAN

iUniverse, Inc.
New York Bloomington

CONTENTS

INTRODUCTION

The caduceus is an ancient symbol that has been associated with many of the Gods from Greek mythology and ancient Egypt. One of the associations is with the Greek/Egyptian God Hermes (Mercury/Thoth). In this association, Hermes is said to have held the caduceus as a staff. In that context, the caduceus was said to represent transcendence to a higher consciousness. When I saw the caduceus, I was drawn to its' symbolism to represent the reincarnation of a life through however many lives it takes to ascend to the realization of God energy, or the evolution of a personality through one life. The staff represents time, love and the essential qualities of existence that are consistent throughout the universe. The serpents are spirit and material existence, winding through each lifetime until they finally come face to face, and the wings represent the ascension to a higher existence. This symbolism brings me to a consideration of the elements that combine to support the evolution of life. The simplification of the relationships between these elements can remove the mystery of complexity that restricts our development and slows our evolution.

1

I believe that even the most complex of entities, when reduced to its' component parts, has simple and fundamental building blocks. If we take command of those building blocks, we can re-arrange them and create a completely different entity. We can see this demonstrated in chemistry through the use of the chart of elements, in construction through the combination of building materials, and we can demonstrate it in the evolution of personality through the examination of the elements that combine to define a personality.

Complexity is a product of belief. When we hold a particular belief, with regard to any specific issue, that belief makes any other belief, with regard to the same issue, very unlikely. Therein lays the complexity. People act in accordance with the truth as they believe it to be.

Christopher Columbus believed that the earth was round at a time when it was popular to believe that the earth was flat. He tried to convince several rulers to finance an expedition to prove his theory, but they all considered him an idiot. Imagine sending ships out to sail around a flat earth. It was foolishness in their minds. He was finally successful at convincing the King and Queen of Spain to finance his experiment, but they are said to have given him three ships that were in dry dock and a crew for each ship that was made up of prisoners from the country's prisons. Now there is an example of resourceful planning. Get rid of useless ships that are clogging your harbors and dozens of prisoners, who you would rather not release in your communities, all at the same time. It is clear what they believed was going to happen. Can we even imagine what history would look like today if Columbus had not made that voyage?

When belief is examined in a more personal context, we see a profound result in its' affect on human behavior. If a person believes that they are not good at taking a test, they struggle with testing situations. If a person thinks they are ugly, they shy away from the light and relationships. If a person thinks they are addicted to drugs, they are helpless when it comes to living without the drug. If a person thinks they cannot speak in a public forum, they will have an anxiety attack if they attempt to speak in front of a public forum. Think about the impact of these thoughts: I am not worthy, I am not very attractive, I am reckless, I don't like vegetables, I like to go fast, I like to get high, I don't do well in school, I am a clown, I'm not very athletic, I am helpless, and on and on and on......

How is it that we arrive at the conclusions we draw about ourselves that determine how we perform in every arena? What is the truth about us and is it really the truth? The adventure created in the pages of this book will take you on a cruise around a world you have come to believe to be flat, a world of self-discovery that identifies the way you became and gives you the tools to become.

Some basic premises are necessary to establish a starting point. These may seem obvious, but anything left unsaid is open to imagination and these premises form the structure for the process that will be developed in the following pages. Reality is reflected in subjective and objective categories. Truth resembles reality in that it has a subjective and an objective manifestation. Objective reality is defined as any material presence that can be measured and quantified, while subjective reality is defined as those things that are identified in thought and are not manifested in the objective world. Objective and subjective truth follow reality in definition. Visualization is an instrument of subjective reality, the product of which we intend to manifest in the objective reality. The successful achievement of this manifestation, and the quality of the product, are a function of the level of skill obtained in the use of the tools that are specific to the chosen medium. The process of converting subjective truth to objective truth is called manifestation. Changing an existing objective truth to another objective truth is called transmutation and transmutation is the process that leads to actualization. A concept is an objective truth that describes a characteristic of quality in the real world in abstract terms. A system is a prescribed set of concepts that are linked together in an intentional way to achieve a desired result. A systemic spiral is a system that revolves through specific steps that guide growth in a controlled direction. I make these definitions here to establish the nature of the material we are working with. The relationships make a necessary distinction in terms that must be clear to manipulate the medium that is created by the elements of personality.

Along with these basic premises, a successful voyage through the adventure in the following pages will require a few things from you. First, you will need to agree that you cannot move up a ladder to the next step if you are unwilling to release your connection to the step you are on. Second, you will need to open your mind to see relationships honestly, and this means all relationships. Thirdly, you will need to accept, and learn to recognize, the difference between systems and performance. Fourthly, you should not move on to the next paragraph until you understand the one you have just read. And lastly, you must be willing to take responsibility to understand and practice each concept as it is introduced.

"Nothing for nothing" is an old prison colloquialism that means simply that nothing is free. The return on your investment will be proportionate to your investment. Enjoy the information in the following pages and you will profit. There is no secret in these pages, no mystery that will confuse or separate you from the "real" world, but there is an epiphany that can change the quality of your life forever.

VISUALIZATION

Visualization is the practice of intention through imagination. Stephen Covey, author of "The Seven Habits of Highly Successful People," has suggested that the highly effective person is one who begins with the end in mind. Since the "end" does not yet exist, and, in many cases, will be unique in some way, the ability to visualize the end result is the key to the successful achievement of it. Visualization allows the creator to build a prototype of their creation completely in their mind. This mental prototype can then be transferred through a medium, with an accuracy that reflects the creators' proficiency with the medium, to a manifestation in the objective world. An artist, a sculptor, or an author, uses visualization to create a subject and then uses their tools to create that subject through their medium. The "vision" is transferred into form through the use of tools that are specific to the medium being used. The sculptor uses chisels and hammers. The painter uses brushes, canvas and paint. The author uses pen and paper.

It is the intent, herein, to use visualization to create a vision of an integrated personality. Personality is the medium that will be used and you are the psychologist, analogous to the artist or sculptor. The tools of personality are visualization, language, communication, logic, intelligence, awareness, conceptual development and systemic development. The product of personality is performance within social, personal, conceptual and systemic realities. An integrated personality is one which recognizes the arena it is in and performs appropriately for each arena. A highly performing integrated personality is one which recognizes the arena that it is in and maximizes performance in an appropriate way in each arena, often leading to the recreation of that arena.

To be the artist with your own personality is to create that personality in the subjective reality and manifest it in the objective reality, over and over again. This can be achieved by creating a vision that is malleable, building a system that nurtures growth so that the vision can be manifested in the real world, and inserting ourselves into the system. Like an artist, we will need to create, step back and evaluate, create some more, evaluate some more and repeat this process until we are adept at the practice of change. Then, through the love that nourishes the process, we can evolve.

Visualization will provide direction for the development of personality, but without structure, and some basic premises, direction can easily meander in a way that will inhibit the achievement of a vision. Structure is a systemic process that enhances evolution and controls direction so that the vision and the product may evolve together. An evolutionary structure is one that revolves in a way that revisits its' premises and vision as it performs and continually modifies the vision, through the use of tools specific to the medium, to move toward a desired end result. We will develop concepts that we will combine in a string to form a process that can be repeated in an evolutionary cycle.

When the Air Force trains their pilots, or the Army trains its' soldiers, they place them in a simulator, or simulated experience, that closely resembles conditions that the trainees will experience in their respective areas of performance. The practice of these conditions makes the actual conditions more manageable. Successful personal visualization is the creation of a simulator that defines you in your mind and then the projection of your "self" into the simulated reality. The accuracy of the simulator, and the power of belief applied to the image, will have a profound effect on the success of the transformation.

An important guideline that must be applied to the development of a vision is that the vision must be created in real time. This means that the vision must develop in the same format as the world appears to the creator. For instance, when you look out into the world, you don't see the world as though in a mirror, or as a movie in which you appear. You see the world from the forward dimension of your physical body to the furthest extent of your visual (actually sensual) acuity. As you learn to visualize your way with intention, you will learn to do this in the same format in which your life actually evolves so that the images that you create can be easily accepted as subjective reality and subsequently manifested in the objective reality. Don't be discouraged if you don't actually "see" anything initially. It often takes time to learn how to concentrate effectively to cause a vision to materialize in your mind. Sometimes there is no picture at all and the "vision" is simply a collection of descriptive comments. This is the reason that the language we use, and the way we use it, are critically important.

As concepts are developed, they will be added to the developing process in a way that crystallizes the initial vision to facilitate evolution. A system will develop that will build motion into the combination of concepts and a developmental path will emerge. This path will interact with concepts as it moves the participant in the direction of their own personal vision. As the participant becomes familiar with the process that develops, the participant will become the artist, sculptor and author in their own life.

The fact is that each of us is already the artist, sculptor and author in our lives. Taking control of the responsibility for those roles, and learning the tools of the trade so that we make this life all that it can be, is a wonderful alternative to seeing ourselves as victims, or products of our environment, that have no hope of breaking out of the bonds created by that environment through the trappings of fate. We are each responsible for who we are, and how we contribute to our community, whether we understand that or not. The sooner we recognize our responsibility and take control of our evolution, the sooner we move toward actualization.

SENSORY PERCEPTION

Babies are born in it. Buddhist monks sit in meditation most of their lives to get back to it. Lao-tzu called it the "Great Integrity." Hermes called it the "All." Many refer to it as "God." Dave Matthews calls it "the space between." It is the first cause, the nameless name, the All that is in all and which all is in. It is everywhere and nowhere at once. It can be known only as the unknown.

From this place, we begin our earthly journey without the benefit, or handicap (as is often the case), of language. The earliest experience of life is appreciated only through the senses; sight, smell, touch, taste and hearing (I would add intuition here, but will examine that sense a little later, for the sake of logic). This sensory perception of the environment is phenomenological, or known through the senses rather than through thought or intuition.

S I Hayakawa, in his book entitled "Language in Thought and Action," says that "The word is not the thing." Hayakawa makes this point to tell us that words are symbolic representations of the things that they are intended to name, but that they are sadly deficient in their attempt to convey the total presence of the thing. The "thing" is a truth. The word, or words, that we use to describe it are relative truth, relative in the sense that they can never be as accurate as the experience of the thing itself.

What is it that brings the Buddhist, or the martial artist, to meditation? What is it that the baby has that people in later years pursue as enlightenment? How is it that words place us in the dark? What can we learn from the absence of language that cannot be learned through the use of it? The answer to these questions has been the subject of volumes of text and uncountable numbers of philosophical arguments. There just isn't enough room in these pages to bring the reader to a complete realization of this place, if that is even possible. What can be done here is to bring the reader through a series of experiences which will illuminate this place and then the essence of the experiences can be woven into a process that will integrate words with experience in a way that enhances personal growth. If we examine the senses more closely, we can design experiences that will clarify this idea.

The sensation of "touch" is neutralized by descriptions of the things we touch. We insulate our external sensors by covering them and/or restricting them to specific tasks, like identifying pain to avoid the occurrence. Peeling back the layers of descriptive rhetoric can expose a pure sensation that does not resemble the words. For instance, take some water and mix it with ordinary dirt until you have a pudding-like substance. Take your shoes and socks off and step into your amalgamation. Don't try to describe what you feel between your toes, just feel it. Step into a pool of water and feel the water as it creeps up your body. Don't try to describe it, just feel it. Make up as many of these exercises as it takes to reacquaint yourself with the sensors located everywhere around the outside, and inside, of your body. Don't think about the experience, just do it.

"Taste" is an easy sensation to experience, but it is underrated and underappreciated, even taken for granted. Interpreting taste is the most difficult of the senses because there is so little language dedicated to taste alone and the language that is dedicated tends to be scientific in nature. You can identify sweet and sour without much difficulty, but what is the taste of a cumquat without the word? How would you describe the taste of a tomato, or a potato? What is the nature of the taste of a steak? What does a heavy mist taste like and what is the taste of a kiss? The absence of volumes of words specifically intended to clarify taste is a clear indication that this sensation has not been given equal value with other sensations that we seem to depend on more heavily. Experiment with this sensation by identifying taste sensations without trying to name them, but by taking care to discriminate equally to appreciate them.

We rely heavily on our sense of "sight" because it is the key to navigation. Spatial integrity affects navigation and personal safety. The loss of sight is considered a severe handicap, but would we consider the loss of taste to be serious (just a tease)? Sight, and the corresponding identification of the objects in our environment, is a huge part of our appreciation of that environment. The identification process, however, once it becomes a concrete procedure, restricts our ability to see "holistically." The practice of seeing a specific tree, for instance, makes it harder to see the forest. This can be dangerous because, once we have trained ourselves to focus on the parts, the whole is lost in the parts. Seeing without looking is an exercise that can expand this awareness. Allow your eyes to absorb everything without naming. See a landscape without identifying any one feature of it. See a room full of people without identifying a single person, even if you know everyone in the room. Combine aesthetics and function to gain a fuller understanding of the "thing," any thing. Refresh your understanding of the meaning of the phrase "A picture is worth a thousand words."

Now create some exercises to see more clearly every day and practice.

"Hearing" is another sense that is taken for granted. It seems that, once we learn what it means to hear, we stop listening. Sounds become either friendly or offensive and lose their relative importance. Separating sounds to properly appreciate them individually, and then combining them to appreciate them collectively, is a process that reacquaints us with the meaning of those sounds and the practice of listening to what we hear. Go to a park in a busy neighborhood, sit on a bench and close your eyes. Separate each sound you hear and let it penetrate your senses. Try not to name the sound, just listen. Let the sounds kind of melt together and listen some more. Put on some headphones and listen to your favorite musicians. Separate the instruments and break down the vocal harmony.

The sensation of "smell" is like hearing in that we tend to lump fragrance into pleasurable and offensive categories and then lose the value of the individual fragrance in the category. Once we learn the meaning of "stink," we tend to cut off the appreciation for anything we place in that offensive category. Every fragrance has a value. The value cannot contribute in an appropriate way if it is labeled offensive and banished from our appreciation. If we eliminate polar categories and attach each smell to the appropriate source and process, we clarify some aspect of our environment in an important and useful way. I can probably conjure up some fragrances with words like pizza and coffee or bacon and eggs, but the challenge is to expand our sense of smell. Step out into the garden and allow every fragrance to drift through your consciousness. No names, only awareness. Go to the bakery and excite your sense of smell. Stand on a busy city street corner and separate the odors. Practice the inclusion of smell in every activity.

I mentioned earlier that I wanted to include "intuition" with the senses, as the "sixth sense," and wanted to place it in a logical location relative to the commonly accepted senses.

I believe that the accurate appreciation of the elements illuminated by each of the five senses, when combined, provide an awareness that places us in harmony with the evolution of events in our environment. More simply, the accurate perception of events at any point in time illuminates the events that occur immediately after. Taken literally, we come to recognize the screeching sound that accompanies locked brakes with the sound of the crash that often follows. At an extremely integrated level, we anticipate the ringing of our phone and we know who is calling. On a more global level, the greater the scope of the information captured by our senses, the greater the scope of the intuited evolution.

Holism is a belief that the whole is greater than the sum of its parts. If we can look at our senses from this point of view, we can see that the sum of our perceptions through our senses gives rise to a greater perception. Neither of our senses, by itself, produces a complete experience. Taste without smell, for instance, produces an experience that is not complete. The same is true of any of the senses when isolated from the others.

The experience of our environment through sensory perception is the most natural experience and the most accurate. Reacquainting with this level of appreciation for the environment improves our ability to understand and interact with that environment. An accurate understanding and appropriate interaction with our environment moves us toward growth in a positive direction with regard to any condition we choose to pursue.

We are going to develop a cycle that will revisit sensory perception with each revolution. It will become increasingly clear that accurate sensory input is a necessary element in the process of evolution. Inaccuracy here will result in frustration because the "real" side of your work is out of focus. Any work that is attempted with distorted information will produce a distorted end result.

Sensory perception is the first of a group of concepts that, when combined in an intentional way, can result in a process for growth and development that is very effective. The process that will combine these concepts is an evolutionary process, partly because it is hard to get anything perfect the first time you do it, and partly because the place we want to go as human beings seems to evolve in an elusive way. I believe that the intentional management of the concepts and the process, however, leads to a quality of life that is far more preferable than the notion that life does it to us and we are simply swept along like logs in a river.

If you have ever tried to perfect anything, you know what I'm talking about. Tiger Woods was not born with an efficient, effective golf swing, or the tenacity and dedication to become the great athlete that he is. The difference between Tiger and Phil is that Phil goes out each day wondering what his game will be like while Tiger goes out and wills his game to be what he says it ought to be.

VERBAL REPRESENTATION

Verbal representation, or language, and its' usage, is the result of an attempt to translate sensory perception into a medium of communication. Verbal translation is important because language is our chosen medium of communication and the accuracy with which we use it determines the quality of that communication. The use of language is affected by a wide range of factors that include culture, geography, history, family, education, timing, perception of experience and personality, just to name a few. The resulting verbal representation is sure to result in environmental distortion and developmental deficiencies because no two sets of these factors, or no two separate human experiences, will ever be exactly the same. The beliefs that we talked about earlier are examples of these environmental distortions. The people and events in our lives inject beliefs about ourselves into our conscious mind and, if we are unaware, these beliefs are generalized, accepted into our subconscious mind and become habits that combine to define our personalities.

We have only to look at witnesses at a crime scene to see an example of the result of this. Five people who see a single event give five differing accounts of the incident and the truth must be synthesized from the parts that are furnished by all those people. Each person's perception is a product of their life experience combined with the physical characteristics of their actual experience, like where they are positioned relative to the event. Our goal is to eliminate distortion altogether, but we enter this process with the understanding that this may not actually be possible.

Environmental distortion occurs when the factors mentioned above interact with the individual to give the individual an inaccurate, or incomplete, verbal representation of a sensory experience. Racial bias is an example of this if you are raised to believe that another race is inferior by nature. You treat members of that race as though they were inferior without even knowing you are doing it. The language that you select in communication with a person of this race will be language that has already built the condescension into your message. If we accept that words are inadequate representations of the things in our environment to begin with, this is an easy concept to grasp. If you begin with a word that fails to completely illuminate the thing it is used to label, then add cultural usage differences, geographical usage differences, historical usage differences, personal values, etc., etc., you see where this is going. I make this point because the use of language will determine success with a part of the process that is developed to shape the evolution of personality. A person can only be as accurate in shaping their development as they are in the use of the tools that they employ to do the shaping.

Developmental deficiency is the result of environmental distortion. When the information that goes into your belief structure is inaccurate, or incomplete, the decisions that depend on that information are also inaccurate and/or incomplete; garbage in, garbage out. A distorted perception of the environment causes an inappropriate response to the environment which, in turn, causes frustration and confusion because the desired result could not be obtained. The degree of distortion determines the degree of deficiency which results in a degree of dysfunction. The end result is a product of the process, which goes something like: sensory perception, translation to verbal representation, use of verbal translation to construct interaction strategy, deployment of interaction strategy, realize product of interaction strategy and reaction to product.

If we begin with sensory perception, and our environmental conditioning has taught us to attend to certain things to a greater extent than other things, then we tend to consciously record those things that we have been taught to assign a higher value. This results in an environmental distortion because all of the sensory material is an equal part of the experience. An example of this might be a child raised in an environment where their parents scream at them and use corporal punishment to discipline. When the child hears the raised voice, they shut down their sensory tools and go into fight or flight. This practice is then generalized over all similar loud, sudden noises and the child has a developmental deficiency. This, in turn, has an effect on the verbal translation of any similar event and can result in situations that are downright dangerous. Sexual, religious and racial discrimination are all examples of this phenomena, too. We treat people in direct proportion to the way we perceive them to be.

I am making an assumption, here, that an accurate perception of our environment gives us a better opportunity to construct a more appropriate interaction strategy, whatever our goal is. If my assumption about accurate perception is correct, then training our senses to open up, to their corresponding qualities in our environment, makes a lot of sense (no pun intended). The more we sensitize ourselves to taste, touch, smell, hearing, sight and intuition, the better our starting point in this thing called growth and the more effectively we progress through our interactions with the objective reality.

The translation of this sensory material is just as critical as the appreciation of it. If the language we employ in translation does not accurately reflect the essence of the sensory material, distortion will result and developmental deficiency can follow. Language, language structure and the structure of thought, however, present some very difficult challenges. The use of words presents issues with ambiguity that begin with the words we choose and continue through sentence structure, paragraph structure, conceptual design and logic, to name a few issues.

Language is ambiguous, voluminous and corrupt. The English language has over 300,000 words, few of which have only one sense, or common use. Lexicography is the practice of making a dictionary. Lexicology is the study of the significance and application of words. A lexicon is a dictionary. A lexicographer is an author of a dictionary. In order to publish a lexicon, a lexicographer polls the entire usage area for a word and writes each meaning, or sense, of each word, in the order that reflects the popularity of each use, after the word in the lexicon. If you open your lexicon to any page and pick a word, you will find its' most common usage, followed by any number of uses that may reflect a use in a specific geographical area or a specialized language for a particular profession. I opened my lexicon to the page containing the word "jam" and found four separate entries for the word with six senses for the first entry, six for the second entry and one each for the third and fourth. That's a relatively simple word. Add to this that many groups intentionally distort the meaning of words, and develop their own system for communication, and this stuff can be terribly ugly. What becomes important is that we approach the use of language in a way that facilitates our lives. This may mean that we will need to learn some unorthodox interpretations of words to negotiate our way through the environment that we choose, but, if we take responsibility for the choice, learning the language is just part of the game. The language we apply to our situations will determine how successfully we negotiate our way to the results we are reaching for.

An example of how language is used can be seen in the mobile telephone. Most people I ask to tell me what it is will tell me it's a mobile phone. When I describe it as a multi-media device that provides voice, video, text, picture, internet and GPS communication, they act as though that's a given, but how would a person know what that device is capable of if you didn't tell them? Now, I suppose that it might be cumbersome to use that definition every time you tell someone what your mobile phone is, but, you see what I mean when I say that the language is deceiving and often taken for granted or assumed to mean something.

Translation to verbal representation is the second concept in out evolutionary system. The more simply we describe our experience, the clearer the description tends to be. Simple language is language that means something very recognizable to you. Color, size, location, movement, relative value and number are all qualities that help description. Add in the taste, feel, smell and sound of the circumstances requiring description and begin to examine the way you put your perceptions in perspective. If your goal is clarity, both for yourself and for anyone you intend to communicate with, the more succinctly and crisply you represent your perception, the greater the possibility that you will be successful in your interactions with your environment. The process does not depend on you alone, however, and herein lays a whole new set of variables.

COMMUNICATION

Interpersonal communication is the transfer of a message from one person to another. Intrapersonal communication is the transfer of information between the conscious and the subconscious mind. Successful communication is a combination of these two endeavors that includes the accurate sensory appreciation of our environment, the accurate translation of that sensory appreciation into a verbal representation of it, and then the packaging of the verbal representation in a context that accurately transfers a message from one person to another. This is the next concept in our evolutionary system.

The interpersonal communication process begins with an idea or event that one person wants to share with another. The initiate formulates the idea in a medium of communication that is common to both people and sends the message. The second person receives the message and assigns meaning to it in the context that was used to shape the message and reacts by validating the message, assuming he understands or returning the message for clarification. If the message requires action, in addition to appreciation, then the receiving person will respond in direct correlation to his understanding of the message.

There are a number of places in this continuum that offer the opportunity for a breakdown in communication. The accuracy of the perception of the initiating individual is the first opportunity. If the initiating individual has an inaccurate, or incomplete, perception of the event or idea that they wish to communicate, the process begins in distortion. The event or idea must then be translated into the medium of communication. Here, again, it is important that the initiate have an accurate perception of the event or idea and then it becomes imperative that the initiate have command of the medium in which they wish to communicate so that their choice of medium components results in an accurate depiction of the event or idea. The initiate must then send the message as a package that includes the proper sensual data as well as the proper verbal data. This means that the sender must use proper verbiage, proper vocal tones and present appropriate body language to package the message accurately. The receiver must then receive the message the way it was intended. This is dependent upon the receivers' perceptual skills, their ability to listen actively, and their ability to translate accurately, taking into consideration the environmental and developmental differences that distort meaning. Listening is the combination of an accurate sensory perception of the message, i.e., visual, aural, tangible, with a holistic appreciation of the circumstances, or context, in which the medium is employed, and the interpretation that the receiver reproduces the message through. Distortion can occur at every step and the message can be lost anywhere along the communication continuum. We have all seen the experiment where a message is whispered to one individual, who whispers it to another and that person to another until, after five or six people have passed the message, the last person shares a message that sounds nothing at all like the one that started with the first person.

In many cases, there is enough flexibility in the message interpretation that anything close will result in a functional understanding and response. The flexibility built into conversational communication allows for distortion and even accepts it as "normal." If that is good enough, then the attempt at communication can be considered a success.

A good model for understanding how all this works is a model from the statistical mathematics environment called a normal bell distribution curve. A statistical appreciation for "normal" under a bell curve means that the majority of people, or average people, will perform in a particular way with regard to any identified behavior. This is the highest point in the bell curve. From this highest, or majority, point, there are deviations of this average behavior in both a positive and a negative direction (Please refer to Figure 1 below). If we take environmental distortion, for instance, and submit it to a statistical evaluation, we would find that the majority of people distort their perception to a moderate degree, just as a result of the distortion built into the process of converting phenomenological cognition to verbally structured cognition. Moving in a positive direction, we would see standard deviations from this "normal" behavior that would approach a five to fifteen percent group of people who minimally distort their perception. Moving in a negative direction, we would see standard deviations that approach a five to fifteen percent group of people who completely distort their perception.

For the process of self-actualization, "normal" is not going to be acceptable. Self-actualization is the process of becoming all that one can be. I emphasize "process" here, because one can never be all that one could be. For the purposes of actualization, accepting normal is not good enough because normal accepts distortion. If you want to be normal in the way you interpret your environment, you should stop reading and put this book down right now. If you understand the gravity of this entire "normal" interpretation, by all means, continue.

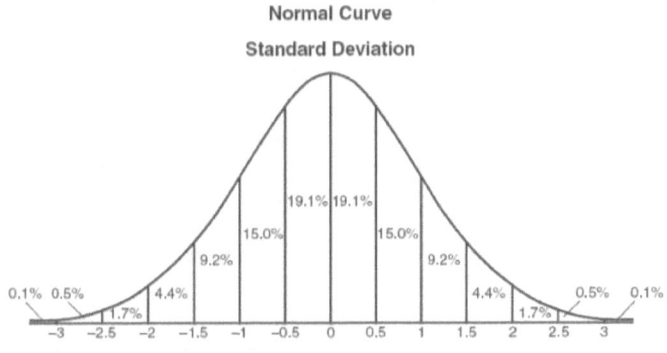

Normal Curve

Standard Deviation

Figure 1

I mentioned earlier that there is an internal communication process that we identified as intrapersonal communication. Actualization depends on the understanding and control of this process. The goal of this intrapersonal communication process is the objective perception of the environment, accurate interpretation of that perception into verbally structured cognition and the development of personality that interacts in the most effective and efficient manner possible as it evolves.

The elements of intrapersonal communication are similar to interpersonal communication in that we use our senses to absorb the qualities of our environment, we translate our sensory perception into language and we interact in a manner that is consistent with our translation of the environment and our beliefs about ourselves, or our personality. This last part of this process, the interaction that is consistent with our translation and our beliefs about ourselves, is the subjective part of the process that we need to understand in order to take control of the process of change. The difficulty with this part of the process is that it is the most malleable and, therefore, the most dangerous and volatile. Sometimes, when you question your belief structure, you shake the very foundation of your life. For some people, this is so frightening that it can result in illness.

You must be able to put reality in perspective, subjectively and objectively, in a way that enables you to intentionally manage the evolution of personality. To do this, we will need to examine reality as it relates to belief.

There are a couple of very important rules, or premises, mentioned earlier, which we need to reiterate before we go on. First, the mind can't tell the difference between fact and fiction. This should become self-evident as you think about it. It's the stuff that individuality is made of. Humans are all essentially the same, yet we hold different beliefs about race, gender, equality, ability, etc., and we all think we're right. Much of what goes into our mind is subjective and, therefore, malleable.

The second premise is that, once we believe something is true, we act like it's the truth. This premise simply follows the one above. If we accept something that isn't necessarily the truth, and believe it to be true, we act as though it were true. This behavior results in what I call a psychological habit. Once we believe something, we don't think about it anymore. Habits are both a convenience and a source of frustration. Because habits allow us to move forward on autopilot, they are convenient. We don't use a lot of energy on autopilot. For the same reason, they can be a source of frustration because, if we develop a habit that is based on distorted information, its' use, although convenient, creates a situation where we are constantly applying a failing set of interventions to the conditions presented in our environment. An example of this might be that we have a psychological habit of defining ourselves as poor communicators. We find ourselves in a situation that calls for good communication skills and we trigger the fight or flight stress response because this is a situation that we are not comfortable with. Public speaking would cause the same response. Is this a necessary truth or a habit born of belief? Can it be changed?

The third premise is that, if we change the way we think, we can change the way we act and, if we change the way we act, we can change the quality of our relationship with our environment. In Zig Ziglers' words, "There are no right or wrong characteristics, no good or bad characteristics. We are where we are because of what has gone into our minds. We change where we are and what we are by changing what goes into our minds." Basically, once we accept something to be true, we just ignore everything that conflicts with it and build our belief structure, which is our reality, around it. Once we do this, everything that relates to this truth is affected by its' relative accuracy.

RATIONALIZATION

The way we think is a reflection of the way we translate our sensory perception into language and then combine that language to develop a strategy to interact with our environment and survive. There are some things that just seem to be no-brainers. You don't put your hand in the flames of a fire, you don't walk across a busy intersection without looking both ways, you don't argue with a police officer while they are writing you a citation, you don't tug on superman's cape (Jim Croce), etc. Actualization fits in this category for me. Evolution is necessary, change is constant. Anything, or anyone, who does not adjust to change will be a victim of it. A desire to be all that you can be is a desire to be proactive with change and to make your life as vibrant as you can make it.

Hans Selye, known as the leading expert in the study of stress, defined stress as any demand made on the body. Of course, he is talking about stress relative to the human condition. If we look at stress more universally, it becomes any set of circumstances that produce, or experience, polarity. The result of stress is what we enjoy as our universe; it is a positive, important thing. Yet, we know that stress has been identified as the source of dis-ease and premature death. I submit to you that the ill effects of stress are the result of dissonance, or disharmony, and that this dissonance is the result of environmental distortion and developmental deficiency. The cure for what we have come to know as psychosomatic illness is harmony. Harmony is the product of an integrated personality. An integrated personality is a personality that senses its' environment accurately, translates its' environment into language effectively and interacts with its' environment efficiently and effectively.

The explanation of the effects of stress on the human condition is contained in the description of the stress response cycle. The stress response cycle begins with the phenomenological experience of a demand, perceived or real, progresses to the translation of that phenomenological experience into language and then the relay of that verbal awareness to the hypothalamus. The hypothalamus is the control center for the autonomic regulatory process. The autonomic regulatory process manages the autonomic nervous system, which is that part of the nervous system that innervates smooth and cardiac muscle and glandular tissues and governs involuntary actions in the sympathetic and parasympathetic nervous system. All this technical stuff simply means that the balance of the body is managed by the stress response cycle, which is affected by the ability to appreciate and translate the environment accurately. If we interpret our environment inefficiently and inaccurately, the message we send to the hypothalamus is distorted. The hypothalamus sends an inaccurate message to the central nervous system and the balance of hormonal secretions and muscular response is disrupted inappropriately. This produces unnecessary wear and tear on the body, dis-ease, and, if generalized over a long period of time, results in illness.

There is never going to be a condition without stress, the idea is catastrophic, stress is holding the universe together, but it is possible to manage stress in an effective, efficient manner, and reduce its' potential to cause harmful results. The ability to effectively and efficiently manage stress depends on the development of an integrated personality. An integrated personality is immersed in its' environment and flows with that environment in a way that can only be described as harmony.

The presence of environmental distortion and developmental deficiency is the cause of dissonance. When environmental distortion and developmental deficiencies are eliminated, the personality integrates and resonance is the result. Is it possible to completely eliminate the negative consequences of stress? I don't see that as realistic in our material world, but the polar extremes of stress are distress and eustress, where distress is a condition of dysfunction brought about by demands and our inability to manage them and eustress is a condition of exhilaration brought about by demands and our ability to manage them effectively. To the extent that we can move away from either extreme and simply interact with our environment comfortably, I believe we can minimize the negative effects of stressors.

Our personal evolution is already the product of our thoughts and beliefs. We act in accordance with the truth as we believe it to be. Belief is the framework that shapes reality. The difference between the path that is defined by the environmental factors that have controlled the process up to this point, and the path that is defined by the intentional structure of thoughts and beliefs, is the difference between environmental determinism and self-determinism. You may either, take a responsible approach to participation in this life and shape your contribution to be what you want it to be, leave it all to life to decide, or find a place that blends the two together, but your beliefs will be instrumental in whichever route you take.

If we leave the development of personality to the environment, we get what the environment gives us. This means that the environmental distortion, mentioned above in the form of cultural, geographical, and familial influences, etc., will determine our ability to perform. If we allow the environment to define us, the process carries us along like that log I mentioned earlier, floating in a river. If we take conscious, intentional control of this process, we decide who we are and at what level we perform, in a shared way with our environment. If our current perception of who we are and what our place is in this world is not in harmony and we are experiencing harmful stress as a result of frustration with our attempts to manage in our environment, the solution is to change our perception of who we are. This means we have to change the way we think.

FOUNDATION

The foundation that is built under a building must be strong enough to hold the weight of the building and the stress of the elements once the building is standing. The foundation upon which we build a personality must be strong enough to hold the weight of the demands placed on that personality and the changes that are presented by the environment. The foundation for personality is a combination of intelligence, the ability to reason effectively, values, principles, habits, attitudes and purpose.

Jean Piaget defines intelligence as the ability to associate and assimilate. The process of association requires a comparison of the circumstances one finds before them with similar circumstances that have been seen, or understood, from earlier experiences, and/or recognizing the relationships between things in your environment. Relative accuracy is an integral part of this process. Assimilation is the acceptance of information from each association into the storage area that defines a persons' reality.

I would like to add discrimination and accommodation to this definition of intelligence. Discrimination is a process of isolating an experience to identify the characteristics specific to that experience before assimilating the information, and accommodation is the ability to adjust to the possibility that the information gathered from an experience may be completely unique, or may result in a completely unique set of conclusions, and may need to be placed in the storage area as information that does not associate with previous information. Discrimination is part of association while accommodation is part of assimilation. Actualization and intrapersonal communication require intelligence. It is an intentional evolution of personality that depends on the ability to see relationships between things and people in a way that makes sense.

All humans have natural intelligence. Intelligence may vary in the way each person is able to apply it, and it is commonly accepted that we don't all possess the same level of intelligence, but there is a lot of evidence to support a conclusion that many of us have a high degree of intelligence but cannot apply it because of environmental distortion. In any case, it is widely accepted that we don't use anywhere near our intellectual capacity as a group. If we can strip away beliefs that limit the use of intelligence, we can realize a greater benefit from the increased use.

The ability to reason effectively means that we have a system we use to evaluate situations and things. This system begins with the sensory appreciation of a situation and/or the intellectual appreciation of situations and things (imagination), the translation of the essential qualities of the sensory and/or intellectual appreciation to a verbal representation, a reasoning process that provides structure for the thought process (association and assimilation), and a decision making system that guides the application of our conclusions. We discussed the sensory appreciation of our environment and the translation of that sensory perception into a verbal representation of it.

31

A good reasoning process is one that is built on logic, formal logic as in Aristotelian or Copian. There isn't enough space or time to properly address logic here, but it is essential to a reasoning process that will take us forward. A good decision making process is equally important and somewhat dependent on a logical reasoning process, but good decisions can be made with a simple procedure that begins with an accurate perception of the issue under assessment, a list that includes every conceivable alternative response and a system that prioritizes the responses for reality testing based on expected outcomes.

There are two basic directions we can take in the application of reason to our lives. The first direction is deductive reasoning. In deductive reasoning, we follow evidence to reach a conclusion, or combine premises to reach a conclusion. The second direction is inductive reasoning. When we use inductive reasoning, we start with the conclusion and think back to the premises that must have existed to create the result. Deductive reasoning requires that the environment give us the circumstances that produce the end result. Inductive reasoning means that the elements are present in the environment, but the end result draws the elements into play. This second direction will be very important as we develop a system of renewal and developmental evolution. We will use the end result to attract the elements that will cause it to manifest.

Values are the things you think are important. Some wise person once said that if you don't stand for something, you'll fall for anything. Values are the things you stand for. If you value family, for instance, the things you do relative to family are those things that you believe will preserve and strengthen family. If you value friendship, you consider the things that will nurture friendship before you act on or interact with a friendship. Values and principles must have short term and long term consideration.

Principles are rules, or codes of conduct, that you adhere to with regard to the way you live your life. Being truthful, to the extent that you understand something to be true, being honorable, being responsible, carrying your own bag of shit, as my professor used to say; these are examples of codes of conduct.

Habits were discussed earlier as things we do without thinking because we've done them so many times that they have become part of our subconscious belief network, or because we adopt a belief that causes them to manifest. Our habits must support the end result that we visualize or they will most certainly contribute to a failure to realize that vision. Psychological habits are formed when we accept something to be true. Once we believe something we act in accordance with it without having to think.

Attitudes are feelings that we develop with regard to things and beliefs, a psychological lean. If we dislike a certain ethnic group, for instance, this is an attitude toward that group. If we dislike certain behaviors, this is an attitude toward behavior. If we like certain animals or games or groups, these are attitudes. Here, again, attitudes must support the successful achievement of our vision. An attitude that distorts the reality of a thing or a belief that prevents movement in a positive direction are restrictive.

Purpose is the reason we do what we do and the reason we are here to begin with. It is inconceivable to me that we could be here by chance. There is a cause for every effect. You have only to examine the effect and the cause will reveal itself. If all creation is the result of cause, beginning with the first cause, then we are an effect that becomes a cause, a reflection of a place along a cause and effect continuum. When you examine the things you cause, this becomes quite clear. It's not so important to me that we all share the same perception of our purpose here. I believe we are all basically the same and that we are all going to the same place, but it doesn't matter what I believe. What we are and where we go is still a matter of the vehicles we employ to get us there and how we use them. If a vehicle is efficient and effective, it will get us where we need to go. The issue then becomes one of quality and time.

These foundation elements combine to determine how successfully a personality interacts with its' environment and how amenable a personality is to growth. If the foundation of a building is not made of the proper materials, is not thick enough, isn't properly backfilled or is placed in a non-supportive location, the building may fall down. So it is, metaphorically, with the elements of personality. If the elements of personality do not combine to provide the foundation to promote successful interaction with the evolving environment, the personality stumbles, stagnates or fails with regard to its' stated goals.

The foundation for a stationary building is designed for permanence in the location of the building. The foundation for personality that is designed for permanence is a ball and chain, an anchor. The human condition is an evolving condition and learning is a characteristic that accompanies evolution. The foundation for personality that is compatible with the nature of the human condition is most effectively a foundation that accommodates, even nurtures, evolution.

If personality is structured so that the elements and systems that are employed to shape its' development and evolution are designed to guide movement intentionally, the personality participates in its' destiny by its' own design.

ACTUALIZATION

The process of actualization is simple, or at least it would be if there was no environmental distortion or developmental deficiency to create confusion. All we have to be able to do is see ourselves as already having whatever it is that we want. Anyway, that's what the proponents of the "Secret" would have us believe. The reality for me is that there is a little more to it. It is important to be able to visualize the end result as though it was already true, but this is, at once, an end result and the beginning of a dynamic process. You would probably not plan a vacation without having a destination in mind, but you certainly wouldn't start that vacation without a plan. You wouldn't plan to complete college without choosing a major, but you can't complete a major without doing the general studies that are required. You can visualize the home you want, but you wouldn't purchase a home without establishing how you will pay for it. You may visualize yourself in an affluent and happy environment, but the vision alone, or even what it attracts, will not result in the end result you want if you don't make adjustments to become that vision.

A key ingredient in all of these plans is the personality that facilitates the end result. It is the personality that creates the reality. If the environment, alone, was going to provide the personality through your life experiences that creates the world you dream of, you would already have it. Folks who believe in determinism would argue that the environment provides the experiences you are here to learn from. I don't take exception to this belief because this book is an experience provided by the environment. What I believe is that determinism does play a part in the evolution of life and so does free will. From the moment that a person takes control of their life, I believe free will interacts with determinism and the individual has a profound effect on the quality of their life experience. The factors that determine the quality of life from this point on are a combination of the natural evolution of the universe and the part the individual chooses to play in that evolution. The way each of us define our personality will determine our success with the quality of life we choose. Personality is the keystone in achievement.

Merriam-Webster defines personality as the complex of characteristics that distinguish an individual. I want to think of personality as the sum of all beliefs one holds about themselves. These beliefs manifest in the way we perform and become the complex of characteristics that distinguish us. The beliefs form our subconscious and conscious habits and attitudes which determine how we behave and perform. If I believe that I cannot walk across a bed of hot coals without getting burnt, the likelihood that I would try to do this is reduced or eliminated.

One of the problems that come with belief is that many people believe that they are all that they can be. Abraham Maslow has suggested, for instance, that the average personality is set by the age of ten and that the only way a person will undergo transformational change after that age is through a significant emotional experience. That may very well explain the "normal" development of personality, but I personally believe that we are here to learn for our entire lives and that our personality is not set until we say it is. Even then, I believe we will see something more that we can be.

I propose that we can develop a system that facilitates continual evolution for our personality and that we can place ourselves within that system to evolve our personality toward whatever it is that we truly desire for our lives to be. If we accept the premises in the preceding chapters, we believe that our current conditions are the result of the beliefs that we currently hold about ourselves and we recognize that there is an environmental bias built into those beliefs. If we want to change our current conditions and we recognize that our personality is the primary determinate of the conditions that currently exist, we know that we will have to examine our current beliefs, perceive them as subjective reality that is interchangeable with other beliefs, and identify the beliefs that will produce the results that we desire.

To begin this process of change, we must first be able to see what our life would look like if it were all we would want it to be. Visualization allows us to experience the end result, as though it were already true, through imagination. We can imagine ourselves in every conceivable situation and visualize the scenario to be what we truly want it to be. An evening with people we love, an encounter with business associates, a sports outing, a personal achievement, anything and everything we want in our lives. We can visualize the way we feel, we can visualize the aesthetic qualities of the location, we can visualize outcomes and we can believe that those end results are real.

You might ask, what happens when what we visualized is not the same as what we experience. This creates a condition called cognitive dissonance, which becomes a motivator to move us toward what we want the most. Before we go any further with this, though, let's examine the other parts of the system we will use to change our lives.

In a real time experience we have a sensory perception that corresponds with each of our senses. Visual stimuli, auditory stimuli, taste, touch and smell stimuli are all a part of our experience, as is our intuition. In our visualization, we must create all of these sensory qualities to enhance, and crystallize, the experience.

At the same time that we are assigning sensory characteristics to our vision, we are translating our vision into language, or a verbal representation of the vision. This is critical because we tend to live in a verbal world more than a sensory world and we need to be very specific in our translation so that we maximize the vision in the translation. By maximize I mean that we make the translation so close to literal that little will be left out after translation.

Translation must then blend into a strategy that determines the nature of our participation in the events that evolve as we have visualized them and reviews our foundation elements to ensure that they contribute to the successful realization of our vision.

The next step in our system is practice. We have visualized, sensitized and translated our new life, and we believe that it is real, now we must act out our vision. I do this in a holistic way and in a situational way. I have a big picture vision for my life and then I visualize situations as they present. My big picture vision is my overall life image. It includes my material, emotional, spiritual and intellectual overview. I then construct a vision for each scenario that presents to me as my life unfolds, many of which are the direct result of my visualization. My practice is an opportunity to live my vision. If I catch myself acting in a way that is not consistent with my new vision, I stop myself, tell myself that this is not me, and adjust my behavior to conform with my vision. If I find myself believing something that prevents me from achieving my vision, I examine the belief and, unless it is an objective reality beyond my ability to change, I replace it with a belief that facilitates the realization of my vision.

The final phase of the system is a follow-up evaluation. This is a comparison between our vision and the actual quality of our experience. If the experience reflects our vision, or to the extent that the experience reflects our vision, we have had a successful experience. To the extent that our experience falls short of our vision, we failed. It's not necessary to identify the behaviors that did not fit the new vision, although this doesn't hurt. It is more important to attach emotion to the vision to create the cognitive dissonance we mentioned earlier. The next cycle will be better focused and, eventually, you will see/feel when you exhibit behavior that does not conform and you will change that behavior on the fly.

The process now returns to the first step, visualization. If there is a need to modify our vision, we do it here. If the failure was because we did not execute properly, there wasn't enough emotion or we need to add something or take something away, we do it here. If we were successful and can see our way to an improvement, we add it here. Keep in mind that, if we want to change direction altogether, we can do it at any time. We then progress through the steps in the system again, taking care to inject improvements as we go. In my mind, this resembles an ascending spiral; see it, feel it, define it, live it and evaluate it. Then repeat the cycle with an emotional focus on the end result, drawing the qualities to you that will take you to that end result as you go. This is the practical application of the communication discussed earlier, refining your personality to produce results that you desire.

Now, there is the system, but, as in any form of construction, there is a foundation under the structure that can't be seen all the time, but must be there or the structure will collapse. I think this is important enough to reiterate again that I identify several fundamental foundation elements for personality. They are, as stated earlier; intelligence, the ability to reason, values, principles, habits, attitudes, purpose and emotion. Habits and attitudes form as a result of your beliefs and performance. Intelligence is a birthright and the ability to reason must be researched. I am not going to tell you what you should value, what principles you should employ, or how much emotion is the right amount of emotion. Figuring all that stuff out is the biggest part of the challenge. I will say that the quality of your achievement will be a direct result of the quality of your foundation. I will also mention that Steven Covey spoke about a "compass that points true north," Ernest Holmes spoke of "right action," I believe that there is an objective truth that reflects harmony with the All. Don't be afraid to change your foundation if you see where it is holding you back. A lack of honesty, for instance, will weaken any foundation because it is a built-in distortion.

When you combine the elements of foundation with the systemic building blocks (concepts), you have a growth spiral that will enable the construction of a life of your choosing. The work is all that is left. This is neither hard work nor time consuming. Once the system is engaged, the changes can come instantaneously. Adjustments can be incorporated on the fly and there is no limit to your achievement unless you build it into your system.

I will caution you that there are always contingencies and the more clearly you see them, the more easily you can manage them. I mentioned the "Secret" earlier, and I don't want to leave that comment isolated like it is. My take on the "Secret" is that the "Law of Attraction" is really an effect as defined in the Law of Cause and Effect that was credited to Hermes in a book called the Kybalion. This book sets out seven universal laws. The Law of Mentalism; the Law of Correspondence; the Law of Vibration; the Law of Polarity; the Law of Rhythm; the Law of Cause and Effect and the Law of Gender. Hermes taught that these laws apply to everything and that nothing can escape their influence. The Law of Mentalism states that everything is mental. The Law of Correspondence states that as above, so below, or that everything is the same on different planes (i.e., God creates through thought, man creates through thought). The Law of Vibration states that everything is vibrating. The frequency of vibration is what holds things together and gives them substance. The Law of Polarity states that everything has a polar opposite. The Law of Rhythm states that there is an ebb and flow in everything. The Law of Cause and Effect states that there is a cause for everything and that every cause has an effect. The Law of Gender states that there is maleness and femaleness in everything. These "Laws" are constant and everything that is given life through thought is subject to their influence. Once the thought is released, the laws guide it to its' inevitable manifestation. Nothing can escape these laws. I find them to be good guidelines for evolution of a vision.

If you remember that everything is mental, you will be free to create. If you remember that thoughts are vibrations, you can change your thoughts and change the vibrations that you send out into your world, both situationally and for your long term vision. This, in turn, changes the vibrations that come back to you. If you recognize that everything has a cause and every cause has an effect, you can be more responsible and intentional in the way you send out thoughts because you understand they will have an effect, just as every behavior has an effect. Attraction is an example of this. If you understand polarity, you know that every thesis has an antithesis and you can choose a thought anywhere along the arc between the poles to create the vibrations you want. Hot and cold are relative, as are love and hate. Each of us get to decide where one ends and the other begins. You will recognize rhythms that develop in the cycles of life. If you join with those rhythms you can redirect them through the harmony you create. Gender is part of everything. A healthy balance between male and female, yin and yang, is a precondition of balance in your life. There is a correspondence between what we live here in the material world and what we experience in the spiritual world. Accommodate this in your visualization and you will feed more than your earthly appetite.

There is one more point that begs to be made and that point is that there is a quality of permanence that must be built into this process. Oprah and Kirstie struggled with their new thinner persona because they didn't let go of the old one. When you begin to recreate, you must re-create. This means that you are not building a new house on an old foundation; you are building a completely new house. The old foundation will not support the new house. Remember that you cannot move up to the next step on a ladder if you are unwilling to leave the step you are on. Permanence here does not mean that you drop everything you believe and start with a blank slate, it means that you let go of the old beliefs in transition to the new. It doesn't mean that you reach for a finite ending, it means that you commit yourself to the change.

RESPONSIBILITY

The word responsibility breaks down into response and ability and literally means that we have the ability to respond as we choose. The word stands for accountability and places our actions squarely on our own shoulders. If you understand responsibility, and you realize that you cannot abdicate responsibility for the things you cause, you know that everything you do causes an effect and that you are accountable for that effect. I don't know about you, but, if I'm accountable, I want control of whatever it is that I cause and I want it to be appropriate for the situation it is cause to effect. I am responsible whether I intentionally cause something or whether it is caused through my behavior unintentionally. It makes better sense to me to intentionally cause and to do this with anticipation of the effect and the responsibility that goes with it. In this way I will be more careful with my decisions, and consider how they impact my ability to achieve the life I choose, before I make them.

We will make mistakes, but the mistakes we make with an intentional, systematic approach to choices will be a vehicle for change and will bring us closer to the harmony we seek.

The system in the preceding pages, when practiced with enthusiasm and diligence, will give us a structure for change and growth in the direction that we choose. Change is inevitable, growth is a choice. The choice to be all that we can be is a decision to raise our consciousness to find human essence, a decision to take this journey called life as far as it can possibly go. This is no place for the weak.

Whether you choose to be all you can be or simply focus on changes that make you more comfortable, the fact remains, you are who you say you are. Enjoy that and make it mean something special.

I wish you the very best in your pursuit of happiness.

CREDITS

There is a long list of people that have contributed to this work in some way and I would be remiss if I didn't list some of them. I took pieces from the work of Hermes Trismestigus, Wayne Dyer, Lao Tzu, Ernest Holmes, Lou Tice, Carl Jung, Jean Piaget, St. Germain, S I Hayakawa, Ueshiba, Hans Selye, Zig Zigler, Emerson, Cope, Glaser, Ellis, Rogers and many others. I need to recognize Trina for her help in maintaining direction with the substance of this work and for inspiration, Danielle for inspiring me to attempt this work, and my mother, Rozella Morgan, for believing in me no matter what. Most of all, I felt inspired by faith in what I have come to know as God.